I'LL WALK with YOU

GIBBS SMITH
TO ENRICH AND INSPIRE HUMANKIND

I'LL WALK with YOU

Words by CAROL LYNN PEARSON Art by JANE SANDERS

IF YOU DON'T WALK AS MOST PEOPLE DO

SOME PEOPLE WALK AWAY FROM YOU.

BUT I WON'T! I WON'T!
I'LL WALK BESIDE AND MATCH YOUR STRIDE.
That's how I'll show my love for you.

Cc Dd Ee Ff Gg Hh Ii Jj Kk Ll Mm N

BUT I WON'T!
I WON'T!
I'LL TALK WITH YOU
AND GIGGLE TOO.

Oo Pp Qq Rr Ss Tt Uu Vv Ww Xx

That's how I'll show my love for you.

IF YOU DON'T LOOK LIKE SOME PEOPLE DO

SOME PEOPLE JUST LOOK DOWN ON YOU.

BUT I WON'T! I WON'T!
I WILL SEE YOU'RE MADE PERFECTLY.
That's how I'll show my love for you.

IF YOU'RE NOT AS YOUNG
AS SOME ARE YOUNG

SOME PEOPLE THINK YOU'RE JUST NO FUN.

BUT I WON'T!
I WON'T!
I'LL LISTEN TO AND
LEARN FROM YOU.

That's how I'll show
my love for you.

IF YOU WERE BORN FAR, FAR AWAY

SOME PEOPLE THINK
YOU SHOULD NOT STAY.

BUT I WON'T! I WON'T!
I KNOW YOU BRING SUCH INTERESTING THINGS.
That's how I'll show my love for you.

IF YOU DON'T PRAY AS SOME PEOPLE PRAY
SOME PEOPLE PRAY YOU'LL GO AWAY.

BUT I WON'T! I WON'T!
WE'RE ALL, I SEE, ONE FAMILY.

That's how I'll show
my love for you.

IF YOU CAN'T BUY
EXPENSIVE STUFF

SOME PEOPLE THINK
YOU'RE NOT GOOD ENOUGH.

BUT I WON'T! I WON'T!
I'LL LOOK INSIDE WHERE TREASURES HIDE.
That's how I'll show my love for you.

IF YOU DON'T LOVE AS SOME PEOPLE DO
SOME PEOPLE THINK
YOUR LOVE'S NOT TRUE.

BUT I WON'T! I WON'T!

I'LL WATCH YOU SHARE, I'LL SEE YOU CARE.

That's how I'll show my love for you.

IF YOU DON'T THINK AS SOME PEOPLE DO

SOME PEOPLE HAVE NO USE FOR YOU.

BUT I WILL! I WILL!

OUR THOUGHTS WILL PLAY AND STAY ALL DAY.

That's how I'll show my love for you.

I'LL WALK WITH YOU AND TALK WITH YOU.

That's how I'll show my love for you.

*To the many who have walked with me
over the years in sunshine and in storm.*
—Carol Lynn Pearson

*For my late husband Howard,
who walks with me always.*
—Jane Sanders

Manufactured in China in March 2023 by Toppan-LeeFung Printing Co.

First Edition

26 25 24 23   9 8 7 6

Text © 2020 Carol Lynn Pearson
Illustrations © 2020 Jane Sanders

Published by
Gibbs Smith
P.O. Box 667
Layton, Utah 84041

1.800.835.4993 orders
www.gibbs-smith.com

Designed by Nicole LaRue

Gibbs Smith books are printed on either recycled, 100% post-consumer waste, FSC-certified papers or on paper produced from sustainable PEFC-certified forest/controlled wood source. Learn more at www.pefc.org.

Library of Congress Control Number: 2019947358

ISBN: 978-1-4236-5395-0